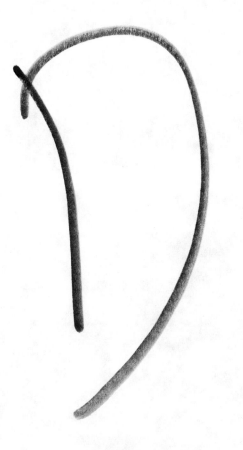

THE SEMINOLES

A First Americans Book

Virginia Driving Hawk Sneve

illustrated by Ronald Himler

Holiday House/New York

ACKNOWLEDGMENTS

The quotations from Osceola, Coacoochee, Neamathla, and Holata Mico are from *The Origin, Progress and Conclusion of the Florida War,* by John T. Sprague, D. Appleton Co., New York, 1848.

The Joe Dan Osceola quotations are from *Osceola: The Unconquered Indian*, by William and Ellen Hartley, Hawthorn Books, Inc., New York, 1973.

The Jo Harjo (Oklahoma Creek) selections are from her poem, "Remember," from *Songs From This Earth on Turtle's Back: Contemporary American Indian Poetry*, introduction by Joseph Bruchac, reprinted by permission of The Greenfield Review Press, Greenfield Center, New York, 1983.

The Louis (Little Coon) Oliver (Oklahoma Muskogee) quote is from his poem, "Empty Kettle," from *Songs From This Earth on Turtle's Back: Contemporary American Indian Poetry*, introduction by Joseph Bruchac, reprinted by permission of The Greenfield Review Press, Greenfield Center, New York, 1983.

The Ya-ka-nes/Patty L. Harjo (Seminole/Seneca) selection is from her poem, "To An Indian Poet," from *Voices of the Rainbow: Contemporary Poetry by American Indians*, edited by Kenneth Rosen, Viking Press, New York, 1975.

Library of Congress Cataloging-in-Publication Data
Sneve, Virginia Driving Hawk.
The Seminoles / Virginia Driving Hawk Sneve ; illustrated by
Ronald Himler.
p.   cm. — (A First Americans book)
Summary: Discusses the history, lifestyle, customs, and current
situation of the Seminoles.
ISBN 0-8234-1112-5
1. Seminole Indians — Juvenile literature.   [1. Seminole Indians.
2. Indians of North America.]   I. Himler, Ronald, ill.   II. Title.
III. Series: Sneve, Virginia Driving Hawk. First Americans book.
E99.S28S64   1994   93-14316   CIP
305.897'3 — dc20

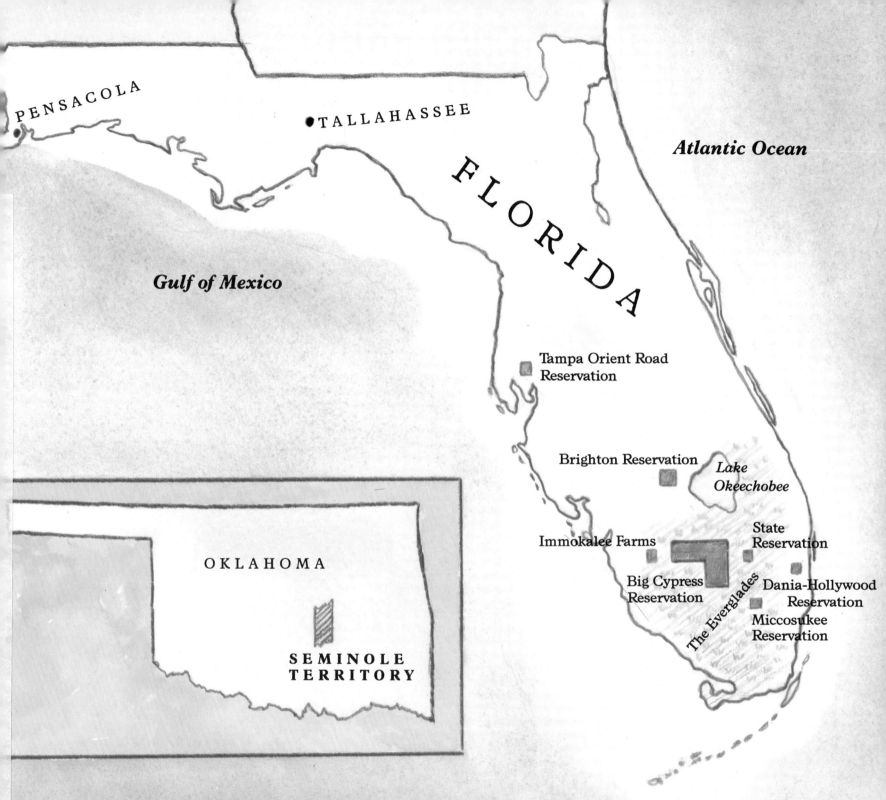

PENSACOLA

•TALLAHASSEE

FLORIDA

Atlantic Ocean

Gulf of Mexico

Tampa Orient Road
Reservation

Brighton Reservation

*Lake
Okeechobee*

OKLAHOMA

Immokalee Farms

State
Reservation

**SEMINOLE
TERRITORY**

Big Cypress
Reservation

Dania-Hollywood
Reservation

The Everglades

Miccosukee
Reservation

Seminole Reservations and Territory Today

CREATION STORY

Remember that you are this universe and that
this universe is you.

JO HARJO

A long ago time when there was only water covering the world, a creature rose from the depths of the sea. This was the turtle. He floated for a long time and grew tired. The Breath Maker took pity on him and gave him a place to rest. As the turtle rested, he took deep breaths and his smooth, rounded back began to crack. From out of the cracks came the people. After the people emerged, the cracks came together in squares, and the people made their homes along the cracks or streams in the earth.

In the Seminoles' creation story, the earth was formed on the back of the turtle.

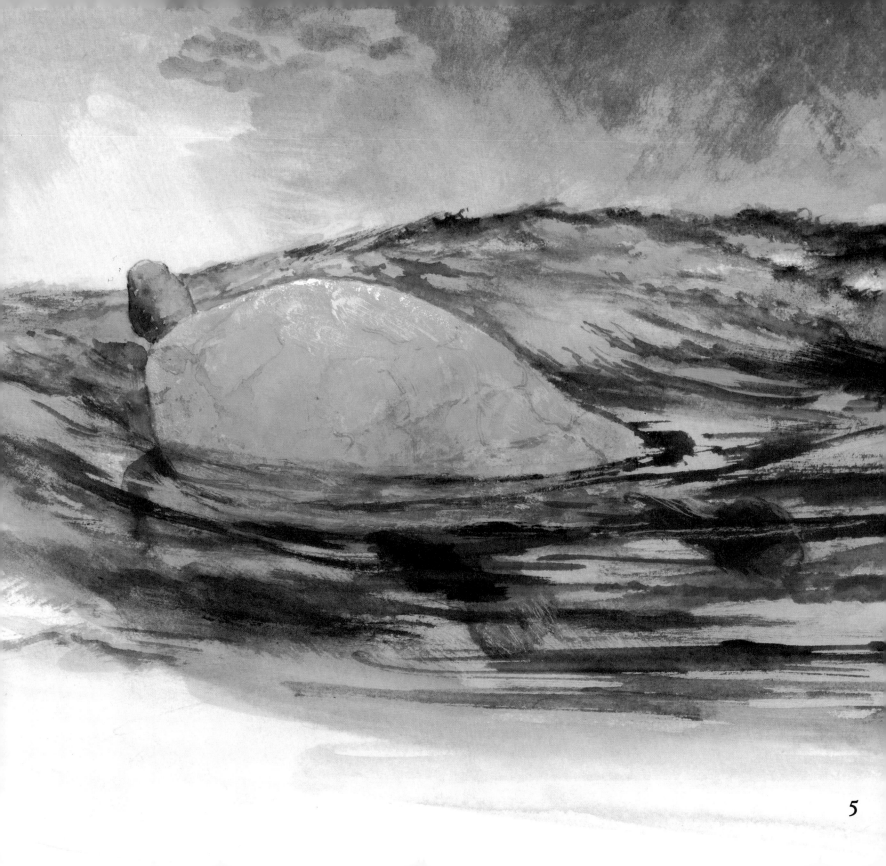

5

THE FIRST SEMINOLES

Why cannot we live here in peace?
COACOOCHEE (WILDCAT)

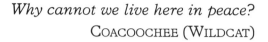

**Opothleyohola
(Creek leader)**

The Seminoles once belonged to the Muskogee tribe that lived along streams in what are now southern Georgia and Alabama. In about 1708 white men came to this country and called these Indians "Creeks" because of where they lived. The white men drove the Creeks away from the streams and took their land. To escape the white men, a group of Indians moved south to territory that later became northern Florida, and settled around what is now Tallahassee. The Creeks called this group "Seminoles" which has been translated as "runaways" or "separatists," but has also been interpreted to mean "lovers of freedom" or "lovers of the wilds." The Seminoles did not want to live among white people, or with other Indians who accepted the white men's way of life.

Burial mounds found on Florida's west coast show that Indians were in the area 10,000 years ago. In the 1500s the Spanish, the first white men to come to Florida, found more than 10,000 Timucua Indians living there. The Spanish killed most of these Indians or sold them as slaves to landowners in Cuba and the West Indies. The remaining few joined the Seminoles.

In northern Florida the Seminoles farmed the rich land and raised horses and cattle they had gotten from the Spanish. The men hunted wild game, and the women made pottery.

The Seminoles built large dugout canoes, sturdy enough for ocean voyages. Some explored the Gulf of Mexico and went as far south as Cuba and the Bahamas. Their fearlessness in exploring unknown places would later help them make a home in the Everglades, a large swampy area in southern Florida.

FIRST SEMINOLE WAR

*That land is mine. I am directed by the powers above
and the powers below to protect and defend it.*

NEAMATHLA

General Andrew Jackson

In 1800 Florida belonged to Spain, and the Seminoles were therefore Spanish citizens. Like the white men, they had black slaves, but they treated their slaves with respect. They allowed the blacks to keep part of the crops they harvested, and many Seminoles married blacks. Because the blacks were treated so well by the Seminoles, runaway slaves from Georgia and Alabama fled to Florida. The blacks had been trained in agriculture on white plantations, and this knowledge helped the Seminole farmers thrive.

In the early 1800s General Andrew Jackson attacked Creek villages in Georgia to get more land for the white settlers. Many of the Creeks fled to their Seminole relatives in Florida. Among them were a young woman and her son, Osceola, who would grow up to become a great Seminole leader.

The white men who took the Creeks' farms wanted their runaway slaves in Florida to be returned. The Seminoles refused to give back these slaves, so the government of Georgia sent troops to hunt them down. Only a few were caught.

8

Since the Seminoles had sided with England during the Revolutionary War (1775–1783), the U.S. government already thought of the Seminoles as enemies. During the War of 1812, fought between the United States and England, Spain allowed English ships to be based in Pensacola. The United States government sent General Andrew Jackson to Florida, where he raided Creek and Seminole villages to keep the Indians from fighting on the side of England. After the war, even though Seminole land was still Spanish territory, white settlers moved into Florida to claim it. The Seminoles were furious and raided the settlers. Again the U.S. government sent General Jackson to Florida. He ordered his troops to burn Indian villages. This was called the First Seminole War. The war ended in 1819.

SECOND SEMINOLE WAR

*We were all made by the same great Father
and are like his children.*

HOLATA MICO

In 1819 Spain sold Florida to the United States. Slave catchers from Georgia and other southern states came to reclaim the slaves who had escaped earlier. The owners not only caught former slaves, but they also took blacks who had been born free in Florida, and even captured mixed-blood and full-blood Seminoles. The Indians and blacks who escaped fled into the swamps.

In 1823 the Seminoles signed a treaty giving up most of their land. They had to leave the good farming country of north Florida and move into a reservation in the central part of the state. Despite the government's promise that the Seminoles would be safe from attacks if they obeyed U.S. laws, they were not safe. More settlers were moving into Florida and wanted Seminole land. They attacked the Indians and destroyed their crops.

The settlers wanted the Seminoles to be moved out of Florida. In 1828 Andrew Jackson, now president of the United States, signed the Indian Removal Act that required all Indians in the southeastern United States to be removed to the Indian Territory, which later became the state of Oklahoma.

The majority of the Seminoles refused to go. They did not want to leave the black slaves who had married into the tribe, nor their mixed-blood children. For seven years the Seminoles resisted by striking at the white soldiers, then vanishing into the swamps where the enemy could not follow. This was the Second Seminole War. It was led by Osceola and Coacoochee who was called Wildcat by the white men.

OSCEOLA AND WILDCAT

I say we must not leave our homes and lands!
OSCEOLA

**Coacoochee
(Wildcat)**

Osceola

Osceola respected the rights of the blacks and mixed-bloods. He met with U.S. government officials in April 1835. They tried to persuade the Seminoles to leave, but Osceola refused to sign the agreement. Instead he pulled out his knife and stabbed it through the paper, showing that he would rather fight than leave the blacks and mixed-bloods. He hid these people in the swamps where they were safe.

Coacoochee was a Florida Seminole who was also concerned with the safety of the blacks. He led Seminole and black warriors in fights with the United States Army.

In 1836, Osceola, Wildcat, and their followers were persuaded to meet with army officers to discuss peace terms. They met with the officers under a white flag, but instead of talking about peace, the soldiers arrested the Indians and the blacks and imprisoned them at Fort Marion in Florida. Wildcat and his men refused to eat. They fasted for six days until they were thin enough to squeeze through the prison bars and escape.

Osceola and Coacoochee being taken prisoner

Osceola was ill at Fort Marion and stayed a prisoner. In 1837 Osceola and his family were taken to Fort Moultrie, South Carolina, where the great leader died one year later.

Now the Seminole tribe was divided. Some surrendered and moved to Oklahoma. Hundreds of this group died on the journey to Indian Territory from illness, poor food, bad weather, and exhaustion. Those who survived were settled at Fort Gibson, Oklahoma.

Wildcat became the leader of the Seminole bands that stayed in Florida. They hid deep in the Everglades where they could not be found. They appeared suddenly to fight the U.S. soldiers, then just as suddenly vanished into the swamps.

After Wildcat's daughter was taken captive by the U.S. Army, Wildcat was finally persuaded to surrender. In 1841 Wildcat, with his band of black and Seminole warriors and their families, was removed to Oklahoma. But when the U.S. government made plans to enslave the blacks in Wildcat's band, he escaped and went to Mexico. The Mexican government gave him and his followers land in exchange for their guarding the border against the Americans. The Seminoles who stayed in Florida isolated themselves in the Everglades.

LIFE IN THE EVERGLADES

*Close to nature, my brother, your thoughts ring softly
on the quiet air . . .*

YA-KA-NES/PATTY L. HARJO

chickees

The Seminoles in Florida explored every part of the Everglades by traveling over the swampy waterways in dugout canoes. They quickly adapted to this swampland called a "river of grass" because of the tall, sharp-edged saw grass that grew in the water. The Everglades covered an area one hundred miles long and seventy miles wide from Lake Okeechobee to the Gulf of Mexico.

Scattered throughout the Everglades were hummocks, dry islands or mounds of rock with rich soil. The Seminoles found that they were good, safe places to live because few white men ventured near them.

Not only did the Everglades protect the Seminoles, but its dense forests provided shelter. The Indians erected *chickees*, open houses thatched with palmetto leaves, that stood about three feet off the ground. The slanting roof gave protection from the sun and rain, and the chickee was pleasantly cool and dry.

The Seminoles planted gardens in the fertile hummock soil. They grew sweet potatoes, pumpkins, melons, and corn, their most important crop.

From the corn the women made hominy by soaking the kernels in water and ashes. They ground the hominy into flour and made *sofkee*, a porridge that was a favorite dish. Another favorite was *coontie*, a kind of pudding made from the ground-up roots of the arrowroot plant.

The Seminoles used palm leaves or shells to hold their food. The women wove baskets from the cane and palmetto stalks that grew in the swamp. Before the Seminoles moved into the Everglades, they had learned to use metal from the Spanish. The women had knives, iron pots, and kettles, but they also used shells for knives and garden hoes.

Each family did its cooking over a big open fire in the center of the village. This fire burned day and night.

SKILLED HUNTERS AND TRADERS

The people in council have agreed.
By their chiefs, they have uttered.
OSCEOLA

Seminole hunter with blowgun

The Seminole men were responsible for defending their people. An especially brave man earned the title of *hadjo*. The leader of each town or village was a *mico* or chief. The leader of a band was called *emathla*. The chiefs could appoint a war chief called *tustenuggee*.

Game was plentiful, and the Seminole men were skilled hunters. They had gotten guns from the Spanish, but after they moved into the Everglades, ammunition was difficult to find, so they snared turkey, ducks, and quail, and small game like rabbits and squirrels. If necessary, they could hunt with a blowgun made from a stalk of cane and darts made from shells or wood.

When the Seminoles hunted deer or bear without a gun, they used a long bow made from hickory. They fashioned arrowheads from the iron or brass they had gotten from the Spanish. They always retrieved the arrowhead after a kill, because the metal was hard to get. When they had to, they used arrowheads made from shell or fish bone.

The Seminoles, like other tribes, had no money, but traded for the things they did not have. The Everglades was filled with alligators, otters, and birds with colorful feathers. The white men brought bees from Europe, and swarms escaped and found shelter in the swamps. The Indians made use of the honey and beeswax. They traded hides, bird pelts and plumage, honey, and wax to the white men for ammunition, beads, metal, and cloth.

CLOTHING

I asked but for a small piece of these lands,
enough to plant and live upon . . .
Coacoochee

"flat roll" hairstyle

The Seminoles dressed differently from other southern Indians such as the Creeks and Choctaws. The style of their clothes was influenced by Spanish cotton garments that were more comfortable than buckskin in the warm Florida climate.

The women made cool, loose-fitting clothes for their families. They wore long skirts and capelike blouses. The men's shirts reached their knees. Both men and women wore leather moccasins and leggings to protect their feet and legs from the sharp grass and spiny plants found in the Everglades.

After the women acquired sewing machines from the white men, they made bright patchwork designs that they sewed into colorful clothing. The women wore necklaces made of several strands of beads. The necklaces looked like a collar around their necks. The women combed their long hair into a wide, flat roll on the top of their heads. The men wore turbans and bandannas.

CHILDREN

You're a Seminole and you come from the heritage of Osceola.
That's what we tell our children . . .

JOE DAN OSCEOLA

Girls spent most of their time with older females and learned how to weave baskets, cook, and sew. Their dresses were not as elaborate as the women's. Older girls cared for toddlers who often wore nothing at all.

The boys wore long shirts until they were old enough to learn to hunt. Then they dressed like the men. A boy was trained by his mother's brother to be a hunter and warrior.

The children had the responsibility of watching over the village fields. During the day, the children drove away the crows and other birds before the birds could eat the freshly sown seeds. After the plants grew, older boys stayed by the gardens all night to keep the raccoons and deer from eating the crops.

The children belonged to their mother's clan. A clan was a group of families that had a common female ancestor. Anyone who married into a family became part of a clan that protected all of its members. Men could have more than one wife. The wives were often from different clans.

CEREMONY

Remember the plants, trees, animal life who all have their tribes,
their families, their histories, too.

JO HARJO

The Seminoles believed that everything had a spirit and must be respected. It was a sacred responsibility to take care of the land that made their lives possible. The Seminoles asked a tree's forgiveness before they cut it down to make a canoe or chickee. When they caught fish or killed game, they begged ahead of time to be pardoned for killing because their families needed food.

The Seminoles were grateful for the good life they found in the Everglades. They knew that the animals, birds, and plants made their life possible. They never took more than the people needed. They showed their respect and gratitude by taking clan names from the turtle, fish, deer, alligator, sweet potato, tiger, bear, wind, and bird.

GREEN CORN DANCE

I can go to the Green Corn Dance, which is my Seminole ritual.
I appreciate this, and I hope my children will do the same.
JOE DAN OSCEOLA

The clans came together once a year to celebrate the Green Corn Dance. It took place when it was time for the corn to ripen. The elders of the clans also met to settle disputes and discuss tribal concerns.

The Green Corn Dance was held to honor the growing season and begin a new year. The Seminoles believed that the ripening green corn was a symbol of life. The corn grew from a seed, and when it was mature, it gave food and life to the Seminoles. Children grew to be responsible men and women in the same way the corn grew and ripened.

To start the year right, the Seminoles had to cleanse their bodies and renew their spirits. They took sweat baths and swallowed the "black drink," a tea from the leaves of a holly plant. After it was drunk, it caused vomiting, which emptied the stomach as well as rid the body of evil.

The Seminoles' homes and villages were freshened. The men repaired and rethatched chickees. The women swept and scrubbed, and washed their cooking utensils. Sometimes the women destroyed their old dishes and made new ones.

The fire in each village was put out except for the one in the village where the dance was held. This fire was the symbol of the Breath Maker and burned day and night throughout the year. The Breath Maker was the giver of life and the greatest good.

If the sacred fire was somehow allowed to die, great harm would come to the tribe. It was only extinguished during the Green Corn Dance. Then a medicine man would call upon the Breath Maker to renew the fire and keep the Seminoles alive.

To kindle the sacred fire, the medicine man followed the same ritual and said the same prayers every year. In the early morning, he placed four logs crosswise to each other and pointing to the north, south, east, and west. On each log he placed an ear of ripe corn. He put dried moss in the center of the logs, then twirled a wooden drill causing friction that ignited the moss. As he twirled the drill, the medicine man prayed to the Breath Maker who sent smoke and then flames to the moss. The medicine man pushed the logs into the flames and then placed the four ears of corn in the fire. From this fire all other Seminole fires were lit.

The Green Corn Ceremony lasted for four or eight days. After the four days, the first logs were burnt to ashes. If the ceremony continued, four new logs were arranged and a new fire kindled in the same way.

On other days of the Green Corn Ceremony, the Seminoles played ball and feasted. Every evening, another fire was lit and the men danced around it, then the women joined in with turtle-shell rattles tied to their legs.

On the final day, the medicine man brought out a Medicine Bundle that contained items sacred to the Breath Maker. The medicine man held the bundle while he prayed to the Breath Maker to bless the people, the crops, and the land. After the blessing, an elder, a respected Seminole man, spoke. He reminded the people that they must remember the old customs, and that they were one people because they shared the sacred fire. The Seminoles then returned to their homes, renewed in body and spirit for another year.

THE SEMINOLE NATION

The white man says I shall go, and he will send people
to make me go . . .

OSCEOLA

Seminole council house, Wewoka, Oklahoma

The Seminoles who had to leave Florida took the Green Corn Dance ceremony with them to Oklahoma in the 1830s. They lived for a while with the Creeks who had been removed from Georgia. Finally, in 1845, land was set aside for the Seminoles, but it wasn't until 1856 that the Oklahoma Seminole Nation was established. There were twenty towns in the Seminole Nation and its capital was at Wewoka, Oklahoma.

The Oklahoma Seminoles could not live off the land as their Florida relatives did in the Everglades. Many Oklahoma Seminoles had to sell their land or parts of it for income they needed to buy food and clothing. After oil was discovered in Oklahoma, only those Seminoles who had remained landowners benefited. Today some of the Seminoles are farmers or hold jobs in Oklahoma towns.

THIRD SEMINOLE WAR

*What we had was a tremendous determination to fight for the
things we believed in — in our freedom, in our land.*

JOE DAN OSCEOLA

**Bolek
(Billy Bowlegs)**

The Seminoles in Florida continued to be harassed by white settlers. The U.S. government kept up its efforts to move them to Oklahoma. In 1855, Bolek, chief of the clans who stayed in Florida, led the Seminoles in a third war against the white settlers. The whites thought "Bolek" sounded like "bowleg" so they called him Billy Bowlegs. Bolek and his warriors fought for three years until the U.S. government offered to pay the Seminoles to leave. But only Billy Bowlegs and 123 others left for Oklahoma.

The Seminoles who remained in Florida earned the name of "the people who never surrendered" during the last Seminole war.

27

THE SEMINOLES TODAY

I never wish to tread upon my land unless I am free.
COACOOCHEE

The Florida Seminoles never signed a formal peace treaty with the United States. Up to the 1920s the Seminoles still lived by hunting, fishing, and farming. Over the years the Seminoles divided into two groups: the Miccosukees and Cow Creek Seminoles or Muskogees.

The Miccosukees' home is the Big Cypress Reservation. The Muskogees' reservation is called Brighton. The Seminole Tribe of Florida, Inc., has its headquarters in Hollywood, Florida, where there is a replica of a traditional chickee village. Seminoles also live on the State and Orient Road Reservations and at Immokalee Farms.

The "river of grass" is no longer as abundant or as large as it once was. The Seminoles can no longer survive living off the bounty of the Everglades. Much of the swampland has been land-filled and covered with the suburban homes of Florida's cities.

Today, Seminole men hunt and fish in the Everglades, but do so as sportsmen. Others serve as guides to white hunters and fishermen, but use airboats, not dugout canoes. Seminoles still farm and raise cattle on their reservations, but they all need other employment in order to support their families. Men and women earn income by selling their beautiful arts and crafts, logging, grass planting, and wrestling alligators. Tribal bingo halls and casinos also provide jobs for the Seminoles. Children attend reservation schools or go to public schools in Florida towns and cities. More and more Seminole young people are going on to college to become doctors, nurses, teachers, lawyers, and engineers.

Both the Oklahoma and Florida Seminoles retain an awareness of the sacredness of the land and teach their children the responsibility of caring for it. Few Seminoles depend on farming for survival, but they still celebrate the Green Corn Dance to cleanse and renew their lives. It is a sacred ritual and is not open to the public. The Seminoles remember that they are still one people who shared a sacred fire.

The Great Spirit has given me legs
to walk over the earth,
hands to aid myself;
eyes to see its ponds, rivers, forests, and game;
then a head with which I think.
The sun shines to warm us
and bring forth our crops,
and the moon brings back the spirits of our
warriors, our fathers, wives, and children.
Why can not we live here in peace?

COACOOCHEE

31

INDEX

animals, respect for, 20

Big Cypress Reservation, 3, 28
"black drink," 21
Blacks, as slaves, 8; marriage with, 8;
   10, 11, 12, 13
blowgun, 16
Bolek (Billy Bowlegs), 26
Breath Maker, 4, 22, 23, 24
Brighton Reservation, 3, 28

canoes/dugout canoes, 7, 14, 20, 29
chickees, 14, 20, 21, 28
chiefs, 16
children, 11, 19, 29
Choctaws, 18
clans, 19, 20, 21, 26
clothing, 18
Coacoochee (Wildcat), 6, 11, 12, 13, 18,
   28, 30
coontie, 15
corn, 15; symbolism of, 21; 23
Cow Creek Seminoles, 21
creation, story of, 4
Creeks, 6, 8, 9, 18, 25

dance, see Green Corn Dance
Dania-Hollywood Reservation, 3, 28

emathla, 16
Everglades, The, 3, 7, 13, 14, 15, 16, 17,
   18, 20, 25, 28, 29

farming, 7, 8, 10, 15, 25, 28, 29
fire, sacred, 15, 22, 23, 24, 29
fishing, 20, 28, 29
flat roll hairstyle, 18
Florida, 3, 6, 7, 8, 9, 10, 11, 12, 13, 14, 18,
   25, 26, 28, 29

food, 13, 15, 20
Fort Gibson, OK, 13
Fort Marion, FL, 12, 13
Fort Moultrie, SC, 13

game/wild game, 7, 16, 17, 20
Georgia, 6, 8, 10, 25
Green Corn Dance, 21–24, 25, 29

hadjo, 16
Harjo, Jo, 20
Hollywood, FL, 3, 28
hummocks, 14, 15
hunting, 7, 16, 17, 19, 20, 28, 29

Immokalee Farms, 3, 28
Indian Removal Act, 11
Indian Territory, 11, 13

Jackson, Andrew, 8, 9, 11

Lake Okeechobee, 3, 14

medicine bundle, 24
medicine man, 22, 23, 24
Miccosukee Reservation, 3
Miccosukees, 28
mico, 16
mixed-bloods, 10, 11, 12
Muskogees, 6, 28

Neamathla, 8

Oklahoma, 3, 25, 29; removal of
   Seminoles to, 11–13, 26
Oklahoma Seminole Nation, 25
Opothleyohola, 6
Osceola, 8, 11, 12, 13, 16, 25
Osceola, Joe Dan, 19, 20

Revolutionary War, 9
"river of grass," 14, 28

Seminoles, and blacks, 8, 10, 11, 12, 13;
   and U.S. government, 8, 9, 10, 11, 12,
   13; meaning of name, 6; moving of to
   Oklahoma, 11, 12, 13, 26; origins of, 6,
   7; Spanish influences on, 7, 8, 16, 17,
   18; today, 28–29
Seminole council house, 25
Seminole Nation, 25
Seminole Reservations, map of, 3
Seminole Territory, map of, 3
Seminole Tribe of Florida, Inc., 28
Seminole War, First, 8–9
Seminole War, Second, 10–13
Seminole War, Third, 26
slaves, 7, 8, 10, 11
sofkee, 15
Spain, 8, 9, 10
State Reservation, 3, 28

Tallahassee, FL, 3, 6
Tampa Orient Road Reservation, 3, 28
Timucua Indians, 7
trading, 17
turtle, in creation story, 4
tustenuggee, 16

U.S. Army, 12, 13
U.S. Government, 9, 10, 12, 26

War of 1812, 9
Wewoka, OK, 25
white men, 6, 7, 8, 9, 11, 14, 17, 26
Wildcat, see Coacoochee

Yakanes/Patty L. Harjo, 14